D1547237

Manic-depressive Pixie Dream Girl

Poems by

Katya Zinn

Manic-depressive Pixie Dream Girl

Copyright © 2022 by Katya Zinn

ISBN: 978-1-7358864-6-6

All rights reserved. No portion of this book may be reproduced in any form without permission from the publisher, except as permitted by U.S. copyright law.

All of these stories are true except the ones that are not. Names of real people have been changed except the ones that have not.

Cover design and layout by Catherine Weiss.

Edited by Story Boyle and Josh Savory.

Formatted by Josh Savory.

www.gameoverbooks.com

For every man who's ever called me 'an adventure'

this book is for you

like the dent in my fore-
head is for
the bathroom cabinet

like capitalism
is for systems of oppression

like mass-media
is for perpetuating them

which is to say
it is not for you:

without you,
it might not exist

but it's *mine*.

You can't have it.

Contents

ACT V.
girl

Epilogue

?

◈

manic

PITCHING A MORE HONEST MANIC PIXIE DREAM GIRL MOVIE

MANIC PIXIE DREAM GIRL says yes to a first date with SAD BOY™ on his third try.[1]

INT. DIMLY-LIT BAR - NIGHT

MANIC PIXIE DREAM GIRL orders a NON-VEGETABLE-BASED ENTRÉE to show us she's a cool girl.

She's a burgers-and-beers-with-the-boys-but-stays-a-size-2 girl.

An unafraid-to-speak-her-mind-but-never-disagrees-with-you girl.

MANIC PIXIE DREAM GIRL talks fast, swears often, laughs too loudly, and drops allusions to a hairpin trigger around unresolved issues with her father (or her ex, or her issues with her father manifested in her relationship with her ex) into unrelated conversation.

EXT. THE WALK HOME - NIGHT

Enter OBJECTIVELY MUNDANE STIMULUS: a windswept plastic bag.

MANIC PIXIE DREAM GIRL, connected to SAD BOY at EARBUD, sheds a single tear.[2]

Set to acoustic guitar and the raspy vocals of the artist behind DIEGETIC AUDIO TBD:

> MPDG
> There's something like... hauntingly
> beautiful about airborne garbage

BEGIN FALLING-IN-LOVE MONTAGE[3]:

—MANIC PIXIE DREAM GIRL and SAD BOY seated
together on a park bench beside a duck pond.
Smiling shyly, MANIC PIXIE DREAM GIRL places
OVERSIZE RETRO HEADPHONES over SAD BOY's ears.

—MANIC PIXIE DREAM GIRL, wearing OVERALLS and a
LOOSE PONYTAIL, paints over the GREY WALLS of
SAD BOY'S bedroom. A splotch of CANARY YELLOW
lands on SAD BOY'S tie. His jaw drops.

—MANIC PIXIE DREAM GIRL and SAD BOY making
S'MORES by a BONFIRE at dusk. He gets so lost
in her eyes as she points out constellations,
he forgets about his MARSHMALLOW. It bursts
into flames and they blow it out together.

—SAD BOY snatches the PAINT BUCKET from a
guilty-looking MANIC PIXIE DREAM GIRL and
douses her in retaliation. They have a laughing
paint fight, ending in a slippery makeout on the
floor.

END MONTAGE.

EXT. SMALL TOWN GROCERY STORE - DUSK

SAD BOY pulls some patented Sad Boy Shit™.

MANIC PIXIE DREAM GIRL finally gets her
monologue.

MPDG

This is the scene where I have the
disproportionate reaction to your
innocent fuck up, right? Here's the
callback to our first date, where
I gave you some mysterious warning
not to do whatever you just did,
and here's where I shout at you
in the rain in a public place,
make a scene, and you tell me I'm
being irrational. Here's where my
tragic backstory finally comes out,
between raindrops. But this tragic
backstory, it doesn't really belong
to me. This is all yours now. A plot
point. So take it.

Take all of it, and then try to tell
me you don't fetishize my sadness.
That you don't get off on my crazy.
Because the truth is, while we've
all been pretending this is about
me fixing you, you thought you could
fix me. You thought you'd prove I'm
worthy by proving I'm worthy of you.
Worthy enough to fix you, right?

Like it's been such a fucking
privilege matching my lipstick to
the shade of your red flags.

Enter WASPY CARDIGAN MOM. Scandalized at the
profanity, she clutches her PEARLS in one hand,
a handle-less brown PAPER BAG of produce[4] in
the other.

                    MPDG
        (to WASPY CARDIGAN MOM, with attitude)

                Oh, bite me, Karen.

A CAR HORN BLARES in the distance.

                    MPDG
        And sure, you might want to fix me
        now, but the truth is, you need me
        broken or this stops being about
        you.

        You wanna tell me I live in my
        own little world? Fine. Then get
        the fuck out of it. Have you ever
        considered that maybe everything I
        am might be for some reason other
        than your benefit?

        That maybe I built this little world
        as a place to belong to myself, not
        some fucking Sad Boy Resort for you
        to check into when the real world
        gets too hard? That maybe I've lived
        on the edge all this time because I
        didn't care if I fell off?

        Recklessness isn't a quirk, asshole.
        It's survival. I never counted on
        making it this far, and now I'm just
        trying to figure it out as I go.

        I don't want to be your vacation.
        Stop spinning my bad decisions

into these derivative-ass lessons on living in the moment.

Stop putting me on a fucking pedestal and then acting all shocked when I want to jump off.

And for the love of Christ, stop calling me an adventure.

                    SAD BOY
[redacted][5]

                    MPDG
Because adventures always end. Once the quest is completed, once the Ring, or the last Horcrux, or the Death Star is destroyed, you get to fuck off somewhere quiet and comfortable and I'm still here.

Once you've hefted my baggage just to show how strong you've become, you get to toss it on the sidewalk at my feet and go off in search of someone with none.

You know, one of those Other Girls™ with those silly demands you used to hate, like emotional investment, mutual respect, enthusiastic consent. All the things I never thought myself lovable enough to ask for.

And after you walk away saying you're too broken to give those things to anyone, you'll manage to, for her.

It's almost like telling someone their most attractive quality is the way they allow you to treat them, isn't a fucking compliment.

SAD BOY rubs his stubble sadly.[6]

                    MPDG
And I get why you'll never pick me in the end. Nobody wants a continuous adventure; it's too much. And that's what you'll call me: too much.

You'll tell me you love me for who I am and then make me constantly apologize for being that.

Because the truth is, you don't love me for who I am. You don't even know who I am. You want the smudged-eyeliner-almost-brokenness, but you don't want the jagged edges.

You want the haunted eyes without the flashbacks.

You want the tiny vintage dresses without the eating disorder.

You want me broken.

You want the depth without the holes.

Because deep down you're afraid if I put all my pieces back together I could build something bigger than you.

I don't want to be "the adventure" anymore. Can't you see that? I want to be the home you return to.

    (pause)

I want to be my own home.

                    END.

MANIC PIXIE DREAM GIRL PRODUCTION NOTES

1. This shows us she's strong-willed and independent, but not where it gets in the way of the plot.

2. Here, we conflate situationally-inappropriate emotional responses with emotional depth and try to pass it off as three-dimensionality.

3. In which we make a self-conscious attempt at self-awareness through an ironic soundtrack

4. Grocery bag includes several loose, ripe tomatoes and two unwrapped baguettes protruding vertically, as clearly this is how everyone does their shopping.

5. Due to ongoing litigation of a class action copyright infringement lawsuit filed by the producers of such classics as *500 Days of Summer*, *Elizabethtown*, and *Garden State*, SAD BOY'S lines have been temporarily redacted until such a time as our deposition proves his dialogue is not plagiarism, but lazy execution of a trope-horse-corpse that still shits out money no matter how hard we beat it.

6. Here, we can tell that SAD BOY™ is sad because of the raindrops that have landed strategically on his cheeks, although SAD BOY™ is not actually crying (nor would he, or this would detract from his rugged SAD BOY™ masculinity).

A Former Gifted Kid's Guide to Channeling Your Inner Chaos into Productivity!

1. Keep marshmallows in your glove compartment!
2. A 9x12 spiral-bound calendar in your backpack!
3. Tell everyone you're single by choice!
4. Tell yourself it's your choice!
5. Fill that calendar until you have no other choice!
6. Who needs a date when you have 365 of them on you at all times
      & zero free time??
7. Don't take self-care† advice from anyone who had pharmacy-brand
marshmallows° for breakfast on their way to class* this morning

*there's no academic accolade for learning the difference between worth
and utility, depression and laziness,
artistic process and savage perfectionism**

**Creation & destruction are not opposites but parts of a whole.
Self-destruction is just creativity we can't let escape us 'til it's good enough.
The only time I've looked good enough is in my reflection on trophies.
†The closest I get to self-care is reasonable assurance I'll survive myself
at my most destructive.

°I read somewhere marshmallows get their gelatinous texture
from ground-up horses.
& isn't that the same as self-care?
pressurized violence repackaged
as sweet, soft comfort?

***The eating habits of an unsupervised eight-year-old at a birthday
party‡ feel like self-care!
or at least like accepting starvation is not.

†& it feels like self-care
this liminal existence disguised as acceptance
that nothing I've ever wanted to keep seems to last very long

& it feels like self-care
this game of how bad can I make everything before I make changes?
this game I'm playing with myself but I'm still managing to be losing

& it feels like self-care
to overthink, to bar feeling
& keep moving to bar thinking & keep moving the bar
to self-acceptance above every success
'til I catch myself
sobbing into a Smirnoff Ice on a Wednesday afternoon
because I have to drink both to numb myself
& to feel anything at all
& isn't it ironic
how quickly the things we do to stay alive
become the things stopping us from living?

      ‡Once, I survived a November fortnight
on pills, cigarettes
        & waxy festive chocolates
gutted from one end
   of the Trader Joe's advent calendar§ in my passenger seat

reduced to decorative cardboard shell &
bereavements of plastic
still wearing the bottom half
of a shipping envelope tattooed
in my mother's handwriting, with an address
it never saw beyond the mailbox because

8. Home
   is just a place where you sleep a few hours at night with the TV on
      knowing you'll be washed clean
     of this place by morning,
      knowing you can scrub yourself

like dry rot from the baseboards, when all the stillness

& the silence you've left waiting at the doorway
            crashes forward all at once
                        like days full of chocolateΔ
                        into the dashboard at a sudden—
                                    Stop.

The self-care I need is learning how to properly use a calendar:
            to crush time between my teeth in digestible fragments
            & take it off of my shoulders

to let go of being Gifted
& learn to be Present
            look behind hollowed-out yesterdays Δmissing
            sweetness destroyed within my head & see

9. Time
            is not marked by empty places

                        but §windows
                        to a background illustration
I'm seeing more of everyday
            & I have so much left to unpack
                        so many nutritional decisions to regret
                        so much life
                        to tear
                                    & bite
                                                & swallow

                                    before I can even tell you
                                    what it could be.

Salt Lake City, UT has the world's largest collection of horned dinosaur fossils

My first thought (when they sectioned me)
was *this psychiatrist kinda looks like cheese.*
His face was round & white & porous

like one of those little Babybel wheels
I used to take to school in my Harry Potter lunchbox
where I'd warm the wax in my hands
& mold myself a matching scar. This
is not the scar he spoke of when he said, *Tell me*

why do you think you're here?
what I wanted to say was

a) because strangers keep reminding me *Happiness can be found*
in the darkest of times if I only remember to turn on a light! &
b) they try to pass that off as a Dumbledore quote when
c) it's only said in the movies &
d) *Book* Dumbledore would never have said that
because Book Dumbledore would know
e) they don't use electricity in the wizarding world,
so there's nothing to turn on or off (with the possible exception of
f) a deluminator,
but that is a unique magical artifact of his own design
& it doesn't make light;
it just borrows light from nearby streetlamps &
g) borrowed lamplight never stopped a dementor &
h)ow can you even talk to me about light when
i) only know it exists
              because everything I see
              is in shadow?

Instead I said, *I dunno*
this is, like, where the ambulance dropped me off.

& I smirked as he scowled

deploring my attitude *(I'm trying to help you—*
quit biting my head off)
& I said *I'm sorry*

it just…looks…so tasty. Next,
                    he asked about my dreams, right?
& what I wanted to say was *I dream about car accidents.*
I dream
about swift turns on bumpy highways. *Can you picture it?*

> *Can you picture*
> *that one*
>   *twitch*
> *of a loosening wrist*
> *that could send your car collapsing*
> *like the bellows of an accordion*
> *into the guardrail?*
> *Can you hear*
> *the grinding scream of shattered glass & the sickening CRuNcH*
>   *of crumpling metal*
> *& the useless billowing of an airbag against an empty seat as you*
>   *f l y*
> *through your windshield like a glorious bird at 90 miles an hour*
>   *& in that moment…*
>   *you'd be so free?*

                                        No?

Instead I said *Sometimes, I dream about flying*
& I rolled my eyes like I expected to find a will to live
*Leviosa'*d on the ceiling & when he asked
why I wasn't listening what I wanted to say was *all I hear*
is the deafening
        thud
of my head
        against a door that I
Can. Not. Open.

& maybe some things
were just made to be broken. & some days when I can't
Reparo myself back together
& I'll think of the time

    my brother's wife Heather took us to a museum
    of natural history
    & the man on TV said
    it's still such a mystery, that what died long ago
            can stay perfectly preserved
    & he said it's what that triceratops
    deserved: to be excavated & cleaned & pieced
    together with wire, so that we could stand
    on his funeral bier
         & hear how they sculpted his image
         from fragments of bone, to display
    him behind a velvet rope all alone

        & that is a comfort that I've never known

because when that paramedic named Sam
threw my lifeless body
in his wailing white van, he ignored the plea I'd scrawled
on my hand. Jammed
the tube down my throat & didn't even wait
to read the letters spelling out

DO NOT RESUSCITATE.

    Sam,
        they're not wrong when they call you a hero; you are.

           You help people heal, and a ton of them
                owe you their lives. I
    just never asked
    to be one of them.

on avoidance

i've left the check-engine light on my dashboard
twinkling since july
a problem's not really a problem
until it keeps you still.

a shrink asks what
avoidance means to me. I ask if she means
in the prescriptivist denotation or
the descriptivist connotation & she
postulates i utilize inordinate quantities
of sesquipedalian vocabulary
to curtail discourse i am
disinclined to entertain

so i replace feeling with thinking,
replace thinking with work,
replace work with sleep,
replace sleep with caffeine,
& she asks me how much longer
i can live on borrowed time.
    i tell her a string
    stretched taut
    stays standing through
    constant stress:
    pulled
    with enough force,
    you'd never notice
    how limp are its insides; how frail
    how it could collapse on itself
    at any
    structureless second. sometimes,
    people ask me
    why i can't relax, i tell them
"because I don't know
how to unwind
without
unraveling."

Diagnostic assessment for when you already have too many diagnoses

after Myles Taylor / after Tim P

<u>Instructions</u>

Answer the following questions as honestly as you are capable of being. For the most precise diagnosis, we recommend removing all defensive materials in advance, including but not limited to: hair, skin, clothing, and sense of humor.

1. *How pathetic is your life?*
   answer on a scale from "My future's so bright I had to google 'where to get sunglasses for my sunglasses'"

   to, "I typed 'where to get,' in the search bar, and Google auto-completed 'drugs when you have no more friends'

2. *Are you an indecisive person?*
   a. yes
   b. no
   c. I can be prone to analysis/paralysis, while at other times decisive to the point of obstinacy, so the answer depends more on situational context than this false duality presupposing a static mindset.

3. *Would you describe yourself as compulsive?*
   answer on a scale from "a tornado may change direction, but never its nature"

   to "I'd describe myself as bothered by Question 2's irresponsible diversion into multiple-choice format"

4. *How self-aware are you?*
   answer on a scale from "I joke about my flaws so I can point them out before others have the chance"

   to "I answered 'c' for #2."

5.   *Do you struggle to focus on tasks?*
     answer on a scale from "the pelican spider finds other spiders'
     webs by tracing single gossamer strands from beginning to end"

     to "I'll get back to you, I'm looking up fun and interesting
     facts about spiders"

6.   *Do you struggle with memory loss?*
     answer on a scale from "In 1999, Forrest Bourke wore a white
     knit pullover embroidered with red and blue balloons on picture
     day in first grade"

     to "what was the question?"

7.   *Are you afraid of being vulnerable?*
     answer on a scale from, "I *perform* my most intimate self-
     reflections for *strangers, professionally*"

     to, "I perform my most intimate reflections of self-hood for
     strangers, professionally"

8.   *Do you struggle with memory loss?*
     answer on a scale from, "No, I've got it down by now"

     to "Gotcha, I answered that already"

9.   *Are diagnostic tools supposed to be this meta?*
     answer on a scale from "The Zinn law of first drafts states that
     every poem is longer than it needs to be, even after taking into
     account the Zinn law of first drafts"

     to "I joke about my flaws so I can point them out before others
     have the chance"

11. *Do you believe you are self-centered?*
    answer on a scale from "my only reprieve from the misery of the world is my insignificance within it"

    to "I wrote a new diagnostic assessment because my dysfunction is too complex for the field of modern psychotherapy"

12. *Do you believe you can be helped?*
    answer on a scale from "I mean, whatever I'm doing isn't working"

    to "I wrote a new diagnostic assessment because my dysfunction is too complex for the field of modern psychotherapy"

13. *Wait. What if I identify with multiple answers to a question?*
    answer on a scale from "neurodivergency is not about inhabiting one extreme on the spectrum of human consciousness, but inhabiting many often polarizing extremes simultaneously"

    to "diagnostic assessment is intended to pathologize every human experience of emotion, until all that's left is a single objective reality determined by whoever holds the clipboard"

14. *Are you superstitious?*
    answer on a scale from "this question exists to prevent this diagnostic assessment from ending on Question 13"

    to "I don't hold superstition...it's bad luck"

in which the author commits blasphemy

the hottest take I have in my arsenal
is Jesus had a Savior complex
resulting from untreated PTSD.
think about it.

>   you told me not to stay the night
>   and I tore my hands on broken glass
>   tripped over a bootlace
>   the streetlamps mocked me
>
>   home
>   at the smallest of hours
>
>   the next time I saw you
>   (my palms bloody tatters
>   holding too fast to something
>   long-shattered) you called
>   them my stigmata
>   and asked if I had plans.

I'd be lying if I said I didn't miss those scars
but my love has never saved anyone—
live long enough, and all your heroes turn to ghosts

and eyes that once saw into you
will slide over you
like a sticker to a wet surface

>   oh, I pretend to love in teaspoons
>   measured doses like it's scarce
>
>   but I am not subtle
>   eventually, you were bound to ask
>
>   how a supply never replenished
>   could be
>   so freely given.

depressive

Pickled

A boy I thought I loved
told me he had a passion
for pickling.

He said it was a great way to store fresh produce.
I took his word for it. I wouldn't know,

stuck as I was on where he finds time for
jars of vegetables soaking in brine, when
so much of mine is swallowed
just existing

resisting urges to resent people
who manage obscure hobbies, like cross-stitch
& philately
& pickling shit

I have no untapped desire for vegetable preservation. I
just envy anyone with motivation for anything
beyond keeping head above water. My mom
keeps saying *we're so glad we got back*
our daughter, but I am afraid

that much like a brine-soaked cucumber,
I've spent so long drowning in chemicals
I've been fundamentally altered.
I've stumbled

& faltered over messes I've made,
over what or why I used to be,
before this sludge seeped
into me. I never wanted

to be trapped in a jar
growing more sour by the minute

but I've forgotten what it's like
to be ripe & alive
& unencumbered: all I know
is what it's like to be uncucumbered: to drift
a little bit further everyday from what you
were meant to be, to wonder
if being shriveled
& bitter is your destiny, to feel it
ooze through
your pores & settle
in your skin—

how do you fight
against something
when you can't tell where it stops
& you begin?

& believe me
when I say that I have fought
but it turns out that cucumber & I
have more in common than I thought
because at the end of the day,
as pathetic as it sounds, what we both want
is just to be back in the ground.
Mom,
I've forgotten what it's like to live
outside of a jar
& I don't know how to tell you
that after awhile it stops feeling like sad
& just starts feeling like tired
tired of moving
        tired of staying still
tired of choking on *I'm fine*s
        & the lonely heat of microwaved meals
tired of sunshine

      & hospital bills
tired of waiting & wasting &
      chasing cheap thrills, just to hold on
      for one more day
      just to not take someone's daughter away

I never wanted to be a pickle
but perhaps, mine's always been a choice—
between collecting dust on a shelf-top somewhere,

or being split open
left to dry
served
before something whole
& well-balanced
like a deli sandwich.

I don't think about that boy so much anymore

but when I do, I like to imagine him alone
in a shuttered manor on a far-flung hillside
with a pantry full of pickles

glowing palely
in the dark like embalmed organs

though I think it more likely
I'd find him beside
something whole
& well-balanced
like a new girl
wearing a scarf she
spent all day crafting

& a smile that she didn't have to.

/graft

strip the bark from a sapling
bind its damp heart to the bare flesh
of another, & wait—

you'll find yourself
a single tree

this is not a metaphor
but my first love language—

the sappy weeping
of truncated parts

half-heartedly begging me
to unlearn.

Hit.

Once a Tinder date told me to punch him in the face.
We were drunk, so I did. He said it was hot
through split lips

is how I like to tell that story:
it lands best this way, all punch-
line, but the truth is, while all I say is honest

I'm lying the whole time.

See, before I got sober
there was this game I played
with every uninvited manhandling

crumpled stowaway trauma
in a rage-tempered fist, cocked
to strike some nearby jawline, lightning-rod
sharp; dull enough
to be played, and that was the game:

> I demurred reluctance as
> he was *asking for it*;
> never suspecting it
> anything but his idea
> to begin with.

I told a friend about the game
once, several relapses ago
on a Sunday drive

(styrofoam coffee in cupholders
from a church basement Home)

shared rites reciting
out wreckages past:

I admitted the first time,
out loud, it existed
(it being the game), but
I don't get it, he said
How do you get someone
to ask you to hit them?

       evening silence in a beat-up Toyota—
       yellow headlights cast foreshadows
       that swam
       in dusty layers across our cheeks

I said, *Power is about becoming*
the freedom a man denies himself

It sounded good to me then,
but I knew nothing of either, and both
of us dead-eyed again by the end
of that summer. It's funny
how the opposite
of both *power* and *freedom*
is *compulsion*

& every addict I know has a habit

of hoarding insights
into human condition
like we're all trying to learn
how to be one.

Masculinity is a prison, and a drug,
he said.

Then he asked me
to punch him in the face.

Thirteen Reasons Why Hollywood needs to stop glamorizing mental illness

1. I read *Thirteen Reasons Why* at age thirteen. That year, I started practicing my tapes in the shower.

2. Lily Collins looked so good starving I researched her preparation for *To The Bone*, calculated her character's BMI, plugged in my own height, and then, using a series of quadratic equations, solved for my new goal weight.

   Two years without a relapse, four years without using algebra.

3. In *Silver Linings Playbook*, Jennifer Lawrence plays a bipolar bisexual, cured of both conditions by Bradley Cooper's dick.

4. In 2017, a San Francisco jury acquitted a rapist whose defense attorney persuaded the jury his victim (diagnosed as bipolar) consented during a fit of hypomanic hypersexuality.

5. In *Thirteen Reasons Why* the novel, Hannah dies of an overdose. In *Thirteen Reasons Why* the show, she takes a dismembered safety razor to her wrists like a toddler with a Capri Sun straw.

6. The month after *Thirteen Reasons Why* hit Netflix, teen suicide rates spiked by 30%.

7. Producers removed one scene in response to backlash. And immediately started on Season 2.

8. Her method wasn't the contagion—it's the entire premise
   Suicide ex machina: only through her death are Hannah's abusers
       held accountable.
   What traumatized teen hasn't fantasized about their death as an
       act of vindication?

9. At the end of *A Beautiful Mind*, Russell Crowe, Nobel Prize in hand, strolls into the sunset, schizophrenic hallucinations dissolving in his wake, proving he doesn't need antipsychotics: he just has to think

really hard with his big smart brain and they go away on their own!

10. People with Borderline Personality Disorder are statistically more
    likely to be victims of violent crime than perpetrators.
    But thanks *Fatal Attraction*, and every hot psycho trope to lick a
    knife onscreen ever since, for convincing the world we're all
    dangerous and impossible to love.

11. Of course they're *just movies*. But they're also most people's only
    image of identities heavy enough without piling on more stigma, so
    why not try to get it right?

12. They don't allow underwire bras in the psych ward.
    & if you expect me to believe even Angelina Jolie's tits look like that
    under a hospital gown, you're the one who's mentally ill.

13. Anyway, *Thanks Hollywood!*
    for reminding us that even through the barred windows
    of the most secure psychiatric facilities,
    the male gaze is still inescapable.

Open letter from a background patient at Arkham Asylum

To everyone watching the movie about the former patient now calling
himself The Joker:

Ask yourself if we really needed another movie
humanizing a violent man.

Do you think we aren't
all shackled to this linoleum silence
by the ghosts of violence too?

A violent man speaks of Trauma, and you call it Origin Story.
I speak of Trauma;
they call it Blame Externalizing.

Ask me how we sleep,
with orderlies' flashlights screaming into our eyeballs every hour.
Ask me when I last saw sun,
or tasted air that didn't burn chemical in my lungs

Outdoor Time is a Level Three privilege.

Count bars of sunlight through the bars on the windows.

I tried to leave this place once.
Three night-nurses pinned my arms to the bedrail,
stuck me. I woke up purple
wrist to elbow.

      they say it's only been three days
      like I've not counted
      every fluorescent sunset since they brought me here.

         but Time's packaged different behind these walls
         here, Time comes in ovals & capsules in two straight lines
         one two three times then bedtime

they scour the hollows of our cheeks for noncompliance

Everyone says the worst part's the screaming
but it's the Going Quiets that keep me awake
overnight they go dead-eyed from defiant.

I am so tired
of *Important National Conversations about Mental
Illness and Trauma*
spearheaded by some murder-clown
with masculinity so fragile
it crystallizes blades at every abuse.

Does he think he's the only one who's ever been made less than human?

      & what of us, who turned the knife only inward?
      who keep our softness safe behind scar tissue?

There are patient files fattened every day here by the echoes of violent men.
Why does he deserve an excuse?
Ask me how many of us have been the victims of someone else's Origin Story.
Ask me about the battered ex-wife
      of the bastard who stabbed his next wife
      who, at Trauma-shares-in-plastic-chairs O'clock
      cried, *If he really loved me*
      he would've killed me too.

Ask me about Annie in 2B, who was an activist
      who keeps to herself
      & has a photo of her dog Jack next to her bed

      who joked about losing Feminist Credentials
      when she went back to Him this time

Just listen. Please. Why won't you listen?

He needed help, that was all,
he needed someone to hear him
he only spoke with his fists
because nobody listened—nobody listened
to his feelings when he was small.

Just listen to me. Please. One more time. Just listen.

Did you see me
while they paraded your protagonist
through the buzzing set of doors, doubled-over
on what the white-coated clipboards call
a *pseudobulbar affect*?

They didn't give me much screentime
but I've been here all along
hunched over dry markers
in this insult to art & rooms
they call the Art Room

I've been working on something for Annie
to hang next to her dog:
it says *Feminist Credentials* at the top
in bright purple marker
& at the bottom in red Reinstated.

Be my witness:
We will leave this place.

I will feel sun on my face again.
I will hear rain
& I will live to see this age of violent men
washed clean from our streets. Ever heard
of a story like that?

& if you did,
would you listen?

Erasure of the short story a guy (who I'd been friends with since high school) wrote, about how I made him a monster by not reciprocating feelings

A██████████████

Chapter█

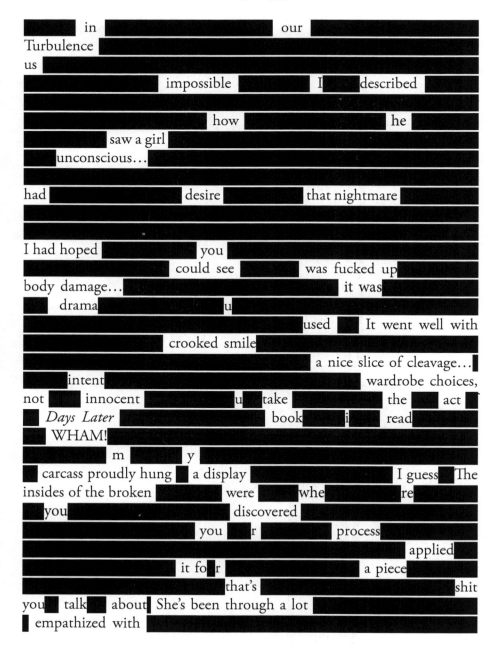

██████ in ████████████████████ our ████████████

Turbulence ████████████████████████████████

us

████████████ impossible ██████ I ████ described ████

██████████ how ████████████████ he

██████ saw a girl ████████████████████████

██ unconscious…████████████████████████

had ████████████ desire ████████ that nightmare ████

I had hoped ████████ you

████████████ could see ████ was fucked up ██

body damage…██████████████████ it was ████

██ drama██████████ u████████████

████████████████ used █ It went well with

████████ crooked smile ████████████████

████████████ a nice slice of cleavage…█

██ intent ████████████████ wardrobe choices,

not ██ innocent ████████ u██ take ████ the ██ act █

██ _Days Later_ ██████████████ book ████ i ███ read

██ WHAM! ████████████████████████████

████████ m ████ y ████████████

██ carcass proudly hung █ a display ████████████ I guess█ The

insides of the broken ████████ were ████ whe██████ re█

█you████████ , ████████ discovered ████████

████████████ you █ r ████ process ████

████████████████████ applied█

████████ it fo█r ████████ a piece ████

████████████ that's ████████████████ shit

you██ talk██ about She's been through a lot ████████

█ empathized with ████████████████████████

inst ability i metaphor like
wild horse broken, galloping
in rehab doing well
u
called it
sobriety cult
I talk, and
invent dumbass things to hear
stories like
I always loved
my millennial Sylvia Plath Seven years,
I believed it
friendship n o t failed
attempts at courtship
There was history
we told each other
our problems. u k n o w
Prufrock, the poem that spoke to u s
for christ's sake
it's no t
about
love H.R. Giger
the artist
weirdo
you're blown away i knew about
I
show ed
u
but o k
her leg pressed against mine with a firmness that
was surely no accident…this i s
reaching
fantasyland crap
I hadn't expected

a kiss

tense   tension

n   o   t   s   a   m   e

u   think   it's   a fucking fairytale   a movie scene

love's a drug   the   analogy is ap   t

I can't

do   drug   s   i   m

addicti   ve

and   you   buy

the   m

in

time   s   I can   t leave

and   it's   fucked up

dream girl   u

called   M   e

the   n

w   r   i   t   e

scene

in which   car   on   highway

ignites   in   flaming wreck

m   e   driving

"manic

pixie dream girl"   be   come   s

bitch. Heroin   e   withdrawal   I   a   m

stupid

selfish

ex-alchie

stock character

you   were my friend

Seven years   but   no guarantee

anything built will last…   only   old

dead writers who

smelled of   cigarettes   s   embrace

this   ending…   this   ambush

you

aren't   bohemian

like   Orwell, Hemingway, Miller,   those dead bastards

Ea   t   As   s

you

love a thing to possess.

I'd never

be the life

you needed I

don't now what

I did t o become

the monster. Perhaps I just

pixie

.

CHUCK E. CHEESE: AN ORIGIN STORY

Chuck E. Cheese: you know his name, not his story
Or perhaps you know not his name at all

You see, Chuck E. Cheese is short for Charles Entertainment Cheese
And he has not just a full legal name, but Dark Origins.

So Charles—and this is true, verified Chuck E. Cheese canon
never knew his parents.
Though we can assume they were also anthropomorphic rodents,
there is no record of his birth to confirm this.

His earliest memories
are of the austere halls of St. Marinara's orphanage
year after year, watching children
with birth certificates and no whiskers
blow out candles on their birthday cakes

while Charles sang along, never daring to speak to existence
the deepest, most desperate desire of his little rat heart:
to learn the day of his birth
so that one day, he, too, might have something to celebrate.

I like to think
(as clearly I've put more thought into this than a well-adjusted adult should)
that in his youth, Charles
showed a certain aptitude for gambling—nurtured
in the buzzing darkness of hole-in-the-wall taverns
& seedy motels, games of Poker
& Hold-em, where money changed hands
under the tables of smoke-filled backrooms.

I like to think this
was how, on what he guessed was close to his 18th birthday,
Charles bought a one-way ticket to the Big City,
leaving St. Marinara's behind in a flick of his bald tail

never looking back...

Now his likeness roams the halls of rat casinos for children worldwide
who trade Victory for holographic stickers & jars of Playdoh,
it is said, to this day...

EVERYTHING IS FUCKING STICKY
& everyday is someone's birthday.

So is Chuck E. Cheese a hero
or simply a lonely rat
clinging to a childhood he never truly had?

Did he want for every child to have a birthday party
or did *he* want to be the one throwing them
& does the difference
                                        matter?

The truest measure of being
is not in what you've had but what you've lost.
Play-doh
is always shaped like missing hands.
Every teacher was once taught they were unteachable.

Giving what you never had is just another way
of pretending it was yours in the first place.
Adulthood is just a way to pretend you've outgrown pretending.
An Origin Story is both the Playdoh
and the hands.

Now, I like to imagine
when the lights go down at Chuck E. Cheese
after the animatronic band shudders to stillness
after the last, sugar-crashing child
sputters out the door like an untied balloon

Charles,
finally alone,
wipes the top layer of gunk from the corner table
lifts a single, stale cupcake from the end of the dessert buffet
draws from his shirt pocket what is left of a striped candle
burned so small he has to take care not to singe his furry fingers as he lights it
and sings,

Happy birthday, dear Charles
happy birthday
to—

me.

Day 1
we were all lost children then.
masquerading as adults while mocking their hypocrisy
we kept streetlamps
& package stores company, swearing
we'd never grow up.

some of us never did.

Day 6
He asked me to sew his shadow back on.
when peter comes back for you it's always the same:
wayward shadows on bedroom walls
he tells you something's missing
a needle will make it whole again.

Day 15
of all the lost children, I liked Ace the best.
he said the world must have plans for us, the shit we survived
and as long as it kept us, we had no choice but to thrive.
so he put down the pixie dust & picked up the books.

Day 17
A year later they found him
in a med school dorm
with a needle
that never gave a vaccine

*you can never go back
if you ever want to leave.*

Day 774
captain hook
had another name once, but nobody knows it now.
we name ourselves what we use to fill

our missing pieces: hook, junkie,
slut, poet, pirate, princess: here,

                        we are all
                        just holes.

Day ?
i tried going back once when i was grown
stood in mermaid lake with a shell to my ear

the crocodile answered; she ticked as she talked.

don't be afraid, lost child
she said, *I have one too*
this yawning emptiness
inside I thought I could fill

with his flesh; no one told me
why people stop lending a hand—
because we always take
more from them than we planned, but

I never meant to be
cold-blooded.
It's just I only feel
warmth when it stays pressed
against me.

Day 47
tick tock tick tock tick tock
do you hear it?

like a funeral drum from distant shores
calling lost children   never growing up
lost   isn't the same as living
                                    forever.

I always thought leaving was something we'd do together.

<u>Day 26</u>
in this land of lost things, how did we not know
        Neverland

                                        never
                                                really

                                        lets
                                                you go?

<u>Day 300</u>
i didn't swallow the watch
but i've watched myself
grow older than I ever planned,
watched the crocodile sob
& said *I understand*
now
I know what it's like
to be the only clock in Neverland.

I know how it hurts
to carry time that should never
have been yours.

<u>Day 28</u>
what is an addiction
but an addled adult's way
of playing *let's pretend?*

<u>Day 0</u>
once,

peter asked me if flying was all i dreamed it would be i said yes
        but i thought if i never looked down i could stay high
        for as long as i wanted i said
        i really thought that i had more
        control here

50

i said   i did not   think

            i would just

                                keep

                  falling.

the rainbow fish retold

long ago, in the land of palinode
there lived a rainbow fish.

her iridescent scales were coveted
by every fish in the sea.
one day, as she was swimming in its depths,
she came upon a clownfish

dear rainbow fish, the clownfish said,
might I have one of your scales
so I may sparkle like you?

and without thinking, the rainbow fish
grabbed a scale from her side
and ripped it from her body

the saltwater stung her raw flesh.
as the clownfish swam away,
a rainbow scale now glittering bright
beside his orange gills.

the rainbow fish swam on
still holding her tender empty spot with one fin
when she came upon a piece of driftwood

and the driftwood said,
I, too, have loved like you did
long ago, when I was whole
they called me Giving Tree
and I loved a boy

who sat in my shade and ate the apples that fell from my branches
and we were happy, for a time.
He asked for the fruit from my limbs, and I was happy to give it
for I loved nothing more than to see him smile.

And when all the fruit was gone, he wanted my branches for lumber.
I gave him everything I had, and when I had nothing left
he tossed what was left of me in the sea to float, and to rot

and the rainbow fish said to the driftwood,
that boy sounds like a dick.

and the driftwood let out
a small bark of laughter
and said,
Perhaps he was.
Or perhaps just human.

Perhaps I was so quick to give him everything
he never noticed I had nothing left.
Perhaps I never believed I was wanted
unless I was needed at the same time.
Whatever the reason, I know better now
than to drift by and let you accept
the kind of love that asks you to carve yourself up
that leaves you with saltwater in open wounds.

so the rainbow fish thanked the driftwood for its counsel
and continued on her way.
before long she met a silver spiny fish
sweet rainbow fish, said he
would you be so kind as to give me one of your scales
to light my way through these dark waters?

and this time the rainbow fish said,
I'm sorry, but I can't do that for you.
I know it gets dark in the depths of these waters
and I'll be a light if you need one when I can
but I need to be whole to do that;
I hope you understand.

And the silver spiny fish said,
I love these boundaries for you

I didn't think of that before,
and I'm sorry if I asked too much.
It does get dark in these depths sometimes
and we all need someone by our side
to be brave.

You have your rainbow scales,
and I have additional genes that express light-sensitive proteins
so I can detect bioluminescence, which will guide us as you light the way.
In fact, as a silver spiny fish, my retinas can detect
up to 38 more shades of blue and green than regular ones.

and the rainbow fish said
What I think you mean
is when nights gets dark,
together, whole,
we make more than a rainbow.

on being asked to write about Joy

I was awake this morning
which in itself is an accomplishment
for me, at least on days I'm not

expected
by people who've only seen me
in costume.

So I threw open shutters to let in
the light, and I thought how Joy
is like my Venetian blinds

(by which I mean they seem simple,
but I can never quite get them to
line up right)

and I've always been too afraid to ask
anyone how
and at this point I'm afraid it's too late to
and now

I'm a whole-ass adult
with my roommate's Red Sox towel push-pinned
over my living room window

because I got so angry with a plastic window shade
for refusing to respond to my needs
I accidentally yanked it from its socket.

Outside, the sky was the
shy blue of almost-spring,

geometric puffs of cloud
like cigarette filters laid flat
framing the arc of a lonely

traveler, and I thought how Joy
is like that airplane

by which I mean my first thought
upon seeing it was
how the fuck did you get there?

Concept: we talk about flying
as this fantastical superpower, like
it's not fully a thing
you can do any day of the week
from Logan to LaGuardia to LAX.

Concept: capitalism
managed to take a concept
as objectively exciting as
flying and make it fucking suck.

Concept: I'm not afraid of flying, per se, but
I am afraid of choosing Delta Airlines
and being dragged
(like every season of *Lost*
after the second plane crash)
from my seat
and thrown out on the tarmac.

Concept: Joy is a state of mind
       (counter concept: in a country I don't have a Visa for
       with constant background checks that bar me from visiting).

Concept: capitalism
takes all our time and sells it back to us in conveniences like,
Today, for just 327 US dollars, you can fly direct from Logan
to LaGuardia and gain 180 additional New York minutes.

Concept: capitalism
makes the people I love spend most of their time miserable
to save up for a future where they can afford not to be.

Concept:
it's easier to blame capitalism for my inability to experience Joy

than admit I'm afraid
that doing so will only worsen the impact
when it inevitably
comes crashing down.

Concept: the airplane
doesn't give a fraction of a fuck
about my understanding of its
internal combustion; it flies
anyway, and maybe Joy
is the same way.

Concept: I was awake this morning,
and I heard Joy
and it sounded like *Get up*.

Look outside. There
is your life. It's waiting

for you at the window

and there's sun
and there are dewdrops
on new crocuses breaking earth washed clean of winter.

There is life
everywhere
and it's all here for you—

every star
and sign
and shithouse rat,
here to drag
and drop
and cradle you

soul-first
into the fantastical
urgency
of Now—

so open your eyes

open the fucking blinds
and live.

on the bathroom wall of a liberal arts college somewhere

YOU CANNOT PROTECT YOURSELF FROM SADNESS
WITHOUT PROTECTING YOURSELF FROM HAPPINESS

You cannot have privacy in this restroom
without being bombarded with platitudinously
obscurontist statements.

You cannot tolerate deep-rooted emotional truths
capable of eroding your internalized psychic armor
without dismissing them as banal
through the same defensive intellectualization
that's inhibiting you from ameliorating the existential torment
you're ultimately terrified of relinquishing
because deep down, you still think suffering
is the only thing that makes you interesting.

I was just trying to pee, yikes.

dream

the astral library

in my library of dreams
the dust motes glitter like fairy planets
& do not make me sneeze

it's the kind of place
we could get lost in for centuries
but I only visit alone

& for once I do not mind it
I have a wizard's cap with stars

& the dictionaries in my library of dreams
don't have the word *lonely* inside them

if I think hard enough about hard-boiled eggs
I can fly all the way to the cathedral shelf

but I keep the rolling ladders anyway
no use but they remind me of you

& then I remember you don't love me
& my skin peels like a christmas orange

so in a sudden, violent need for enclosure
I ask the lollipop man who appears
please, sir, will you keep

half an eye on my sprinkles
for 30 seconds, tops

so I can unravel all the way
inside the bookcase?

& it's not until I wake up in pieces
I see how fucking hysterical it is

that even in an astral body
in a library of dreams,
my subconscious finds it too unrealistic
to ask the man made of icing sugar
for a minute
of his time, uninterrupted

or even
an entire eyeball.

In a parallel universe where it really is a scary time for men

After Olivia Gatwood

I have a question about transpersonal psychology
& when the professor calls on me I do not preface it

with an apology. Here,
I do not have to understand everything
to prove I am not stupid.

Here, I get dressed in all the chunky knits,
a boy once said gave me *this metrofeminist look*
that's, like, unappealing to most men. My arms
distend into purl-stitched weather balloons,
but I do not mind. Here, I am not afraid
to take up space. Here, I do not
jam my shoulders into
my eardrums. Here, I do not stack
my spine on his approval. Here,

I do not build myself smaller
to make his hands look bigger.
Here, I take up space
in every shape of myself.

I go on a first date
& when he lifts my hand
& places it over his crotch
I do not leave it there.

Instead, I take my own hand
(tenderly)
& I punch him in the balls

& that's when I say
Motherfucker, I know where your dick is
and if I wanted to touch it
I would've done it my goddamn self.

When he ghosts me,
I do not fear
my own disappearance. When he ghosts me,
I become a specter
in his daydreams, whisper my own name
in the crevices of his collarbones,
call myself Choice
call myself Still Living.
When he ghosts me,
I let him.

I fill my reasonably-sized pockets
with the periods
of all my newly-finished sentences
and slingshot them
one by one
into the eyeballs
of the male NASA scientists
who sent astronaut Sally Ride
on a 3-day tour of the galaxy
with 100 tampons
and a zero-gravity cosmetic kit.

All the hair and make-up-removing paraphernalia
used by women in commercials form a SAG union.
Demand real work. Their chief spokesrazor
issues a statement:

We are tired
of our blades growing dull skating across skin
already balder than peeled eggs from the eyes down.

Adds their P.R. wipe: *What is the point in hiring us*
to remove only the top layer of foundation?
Why do we teach these bodies

their natural states are
something shameful, indecent?

On a tidal wave of that blue goo
that stars as Blood
in Tampax commercials,
they arrive at the Oscars
& where there are not more actresses
they've seen on-screen naked
than bare-faced.

And the Oscar goes to…
an actress who didn't have to endure
some Charlize-Theron-in-Monster-esque physical transformation
to appear ugly enough to be judged
solely on talent,
but I do not watch.
My Sunday nights

are spent unspooling every flashback
from the mainstage of my brain,
dipping them in newspaper ink
squeezed from every article that ever published

Brock Turner's swimming scores
& tattooing them
on the inner eyelids
of every man who heard *Try harder* when I told him No.

I am told
this is gratuitous
horror.

But the last time I told a man I trusted that I was scared
he took it as an invitation.

Some people
are due for a haunting.

Saying I love you in neurodivergent

Your name in my mouth tastes like smiling.

You're the most beautiful thing I've ever been stuck on.

Remember that niche interest you mentioned two Sundays ago?
Here's a relevant article I'd like to ask you
      17 follow-up questions about.
Some of the answers I already know
but I love the way your eyes get all wide and sparkly
      when you talk about a passion.

I'm not afraid of you
but you scare me.
Did I scare you away?

Do you want to know some fun and interesting facts about snails?

According to some anthropologists, legends of Cupids were inspired by
helix aspersa, a hermaphroditic garden snail. These slimy Casanovas show
interest by shooting dart-shaped snot rockets coated in sperm-fortifying
mucus membranes at passing snails catching their eyestalks.

Did I scare you away yet?

The presence of a protective shell is the only known biological distinction
between snails and slugs.

Did I scare you away yet?

Here's a pocket-sized pop-up book of a poem, based on a text you sent in
2016, made from a lonely blue journal I rescued from a ransacked dollar
bin at a Target last winter. Anyways, Merry Christmas.

You give me the courage to be myself,
which is to say you have Top energy.

I learned that song we both love on the guitar.

Is it rude to say you make me feel like a slug?
Would you tell me if I was scaring you away?

I'm certain I knew you in a life before this one.
My head goes quiet when you call my name.

What's your sun, moon, and rising?
What's the last dream you remember?
I found this on a curb today and thought of you.

Are you sure I haven't scared you away?

I'm not saying you're my Reason
'cause I know better now,
but I'm happy I stayed long enough to know you.

Yorty Creek

You thought it was a woodpecker.

but I always remembered a hummingbird,
and it makes sense, doesn't it?—you,
sturdy, balanced, chipping out slowly
your place in this world, and me—

flighty, wistful, held aloft by whirring frenzy
bursting with nectar tasted only when shared
never known home
as anything less fleeting than a whisper
through tulips, sometimes piercing

but always taut and waiting
to watch the world grow.

I don't know, you said
but I can tell you what I hope
and after that, I admit
I heard nothing

just thrumming
jammed silence
with a shoe-drop thud. I'm
still learning stillness
means more than freefall.

& in this parable of mistakes, you
are the archetype I understand
most and least, and even if all you meant
when you said we were like a dream to you
was eventually we had to wake up,
somehow

I can't regret

a moment wasted believing
in some prophecy or myth:
collision
once, twice
into this fragile infinity
we dared
the fates
themselves had spun of

more
than coincidence.
It has to be,
you said,

the way I'd started, unbidden
this old Navajo fable you heard
as a child, of that brave little bird
whose beak pierced blackness, gave us
the stars we slept under that night.

***

& even in those years we went without
a word between us, you said
knowing I was out there writing poems
to keep myself sane made you smile

& I wonder if you'll ever find out
you became one

***

& if you do,
by the first hole to pierce the sky

blue-black against my windshield,
at every traffic light in this town

I'll pin a wish to see you
smile again.

Robert Frost walks me home on a summer's evening

in conversation with Lip Manegio

A poet friend once asked me
who among us has not made something we love into a metaphor for suicide?

Two miles home from the odd-hours café where I meet my sponsor,
midnight lingers at tenement windows, and streetlamps
begin to glow with starlight urgency.
There's something sacred in these long evening walks I take with myself.

I like to think Robert Frost stopped by *those* woods on that snowy evening
exclusively for leaf-peeping purposes, and scholars
have been analytically jerking each other off about it ever since.

Too often, I am told to be afraid here.

I am told this city is a hunting ground,
the click-burn of oncoming streetlamps
a call of the wild. I am told if I must
walk home here, or leave home here,
or anywhere men are, do it with a knife in my boot
mace on my keychain, thumb
on an app ready to alert police the second I flinch. My friends

compare artillery at the dinner table, show off brass knuckles
shaped like cat ears, switchblade lipstick, keys
wedged in the webbing of their hands
like latchkey Wolverines. We go out at night,

they lace up their combat boots
and prepare for combat.

They see Death everywhere
like English majors with a Robert Frost poem.

I once searched for Death on Friday streetcorners—
teenage emptiness draped in fishnets and leather, mouth painted target

smiling under bluesmoke awnings praying some stubble-jawed stranger
would read my paper-backed vulnerability and make me a hardcover,

crack my spine and with his hands
bring forward
        my ending.

There's a shortcut through the park at Fenway,
streetlamps drip dappled gold through the trees.

> [**A stranger in a van** leans out one tinted window,
> asks where I'm headed in those heels.
> **A man I know from my Thursday-night meeting**
> says roads are unsafe on snowy evenings,
> offers sanctuary of his home]

Pop Quiz: *Using clues found in the above text, which character do you predict will*
    a) assault the speaker
    b) drop them off intact at a train station, saying *Sweetheart, you
don't have to treat yourself like this*

I've had nightmares starring men I trusted
& starred in dreams where I have died.
Robert Frost stared into the woods at night, they say to ponder suicide.
I'm not afraid in these woods alone tonight,
though they say this is how women die

   & I don't know
   if this is a victory
   or a symptom.

I am the most dangerous thing that's ever happened to me,
and I intend to survive myself.

     *There are miles
     to go before I sleep.*

girl

A minor notes

my first piano recital
I played Mozart
wore black velvet

my hair in a French braid
almost long enough to sit on.

Mr. Gevorkian had a funny accent;
the scent of his sweat and cologne

clung to the living room
days after a lesson.
When I hit my notes wrong
he'd squeeze the offending digit

under the thumb of his dominant hand
against the lump of his knuckle
like he was popping a grape

shake the arm attached
up and down till I cried

he never did the same to
my brother.
I never asked him why

Mr. Gevorkian said crying was for babies
he yelled when I flinched at his hands.
In my first-grade journal, in my best printing,
I wrote *he is a nice man but very stict*

the day he walked out on a lesson
saying I had talent but couldn't be taught
I wrote my first concrete poem
in the shape of a great big frown.

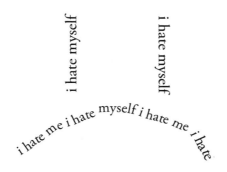

i hate me i hate myself i hate me i hate

looking back now

I'd call it banal
needlessly repetitive without artistic justification

my first piano recital
I wore black velvet
I played Mozart

but Mr. Gevorkian didn't like my hair down
or when my clothes showed too much leg

zey will look to za long, blond hair
or zey will look to za leg
zey will not hear you play
unless za note is sour

my first piano recital
I wore black velvet
I played Mozart

& that was the first time I remember
wondering

if I'd always be looked at
before being seen.

farewell, my honey

past the doorway frowned
wide-open, I beckoned you
inside—jasmine candles

on broken windowsills
turntable, singing
softly by the fireplace

a far gone lullaby…

we slow-danced
barefoot on the hardwood floor
two bodies
spinning sweet & sleepy
to dirges by the dead.

believe
i never meant to hurt you, you
never asked for this, i know—

trauma, my honey,
looks like an unhinged
            front door, jigsaw vinyl records
            shattered picture windows

trauma, my honey,
is the *into* following
broken, but wreckage

is wreckage,
just the same.
        i'm sorry

for the bloody footprints
on your carpet, the jagged splinters

at your feet. forgive the evening breeze
for fluttering my curtain ends
        ablaze.

i'm sorry the best way
i know how to love
looks like so much

bleeding
& burning
i do not expect you

to stay for this
you don't even need
to close the door. it doesn't. i didn't

bother to fix the latch after the last break-in.
it didn't matter much what happened to me—

why face the damage
of someone else's crime?

                but the look on your face
                your sliced-open sole

is all the answer
i'll ever need.

so cut your losses, honey
i'm not afraid this time.

leave me home to sweep
while the stereo weeps

...gonna leave
this brokedown palace
on my hands and knees...

                    intimacy
is an innocent houseguest
i should've known

i wasn't ready
to entertain
i didn't mean

for us to find out this way,
i should've known

better
sooner

but there it is.

bell j(ars poetica)

Sylvia Plath effect: a term coined in 2001 by psychologist Charles C. Kaufman alleging that, of all creative writers, poets are most prone to mental illness.

> here is the best way i know how to explain it
> what if poems are not art
> but possession
> ?
> first, heat
> urgent,
> alive
>
> harder to trap gaseous
> but easiest to release
>
> then,
> liquid
> cooling
>
> slow creep to
> viscous solid
> *let it out*
>
> or it grows sour
> like spoiled milk
> sets thick & heavy
> in your bones
> you'll lose days
> to a prison
> of bed
> watch the sun trickle down
> your window
> mourn past exorcisms whose verse
> seems now
> more foreign than a stranger's—
> *let it out, let it out*

like a medieval doctor
does a ghost of the blood

do you think

when they cut open sylvia plath
the hiss escaping her white, defenseless skin
was poetry gone unwritten
?

or was it
just carbon monoxide

?

After Zelda Fitzgerald, the original Manic Pixie Dream Girl

Did you know that F. Scott Fitzgerald invented the word *orgastic?*

It's true. His vision of Gatsby's imagined future
stretched thus far past confines of prescriptivism:
he birthed this bastard child of *orgiastic* and *orgasmic.*

Despite being remembered mainly for
marrying One of the Greatest American Writers
of the Twentieth Century, Zelda Fitzgerald
was an artist in her own right—

accomplished dancer, talented actress,
gifted writer, motorcycle enthusiast,
certifiably a bad bitch.

Committed to a psychiatric facility in 1930,
her Wikipedia legacy
includes the semi-autobiographical novel *Save Me the Waltz*
and the diagnoses *Hysteria*
and *paranoid schizophrenia.*

     Unmentioned
is the entry in her husband's journal
plotting her psychological destruction as a means of
ending her career: *Attack on all grounds.*

…Detach…Disorient…
Probable result: new breakdown.

or her private journals
from which he stole entire passages
of *The Beautiful and the Damned*

     Unmentioned
the way he forbade her

from accepting starring roles,
publishing contracts, spotlights, from existing
outside the texts he trapped her between
like a flypaper dragonfly, while he plotted
open the uncracked spine
of an underage silent film star
with his influential voice,
called her
his Muse too; called her
his Hollywood dream.

      Unmentioned
is the letter he sent Zelda in the hospital:
      You were going crazy,
      and calling it genius.

Did you know *crazy*
is just a word men use
when they mean inconvenient?

when they mean you have delusions
of independence?
when they mean *I've never made anyone orgastic*
and now it's your fault I have a complex about it.

If F. Scott Fitzgerald
is indeed One of the Greatest American writers
of the Twentieth Century, perhaps
the etymology of violence begins here—
with women remembered by the abuse they endured

& men praised for seeing a hard definition
as invitation for their craft.

Zelda Sayre Fitzgerald died in 1948
in the fire that swallowed Highland Sanitarium.

She could not escape
the flames because
they chained her to the bed.

Today, there is a museum
in the ashes where it stood

some say the walls still whisper *Zelda*
some say it smolders in the dark

the way every femme they call crazy
is a Fire refusing to be put out

the way every femme
men fear
is an endless,

                        burning thing.

An open letter to the parents against teaching children about consent

Dear Moms and Dads going off about "Politics have no place in classroom," like *hands to yourself* suddenly became a political stance,

> Listen.
> When I was 5, the boys on the playground pulled my hair.
> The grown-ups said that meant they liked me.
>
> When I was 8, a boy in my class cornered me
> in the hallway after-school
> to tell me I was *the cutest thing he'd ever seen.*
> I didn't know what to say, so I said nothing, and ran
> to the grassy area where the cars pulled in for pick-up.
> The grown-ups said, *Next time, smile and say thank you.*
> *It's rude not to accept compliments.*
> I didn't mind being called cute.
> > I just didn't like the part where he called me a thing.
>
> When I was 12, a boy in my Algebra class put my pencil case
> down the front of his boxers and refused to give it back
> until the end of fourth period.
> The other kids in my class said, *It's just a joke!*
> *Don't be a bitch.*
> *No one likes a snitch.*
> *But maybe throw away your pencil case, it touched his dick.*
>
> The boy who sat next to me in that same class, said Pencil-Dick
> was a jerk. He'd never do a thing like that.
> He wasn't like the other guys.
> The next day, he left his notebook open on his desk.
> I caught a glimpse of his artwork.
> Two stick-figures labeled with mine and his names.
> Above his was a thought bubble with a 7-digit number and the
> words *Should I call her??*
> It was mine.
> I'd never given it to him.

The boy who sat behind me told me Stick-Figure-Boy had a habit of rubbing strands of my hair between his fingers when I wasn't looking.
My hair was long enough that I never noticed.
I asked him why he never said anything while it happened.
He looked at me like I'd asked him to solve a quadratic equation in his head.

When I was 13, a boy outside the library thought it would be funny to flip me upside-down and swing me in circles by my feet until I was too dizzy to stand.
I told him he was scaring me.
Relax, Barbie Doll, I'm not gonna drop you.
Then he dropped me on my head.

When I was 14, the boy who sat behind me in Honors Social Science reached under my yellow and black flannel and unhooked my bra during the lecture.
Three of my classmates saw. They said *If you ignore him, he'll stop bothering you*
He didn't.

When I was 14, the boys in Drama thought it was funny to tickle me until I lost control of my limbs and fell on the ground.
A girl in my class looked down at me, smirking. *It's because you like the attention.*

When I was 15, I practiced a dance for P.E. in a white tank top.
When I got home, I had a message from a boy in my class demanding I stop wearing "see-through outfits" to school because he was having trouble keeping his reaction in his shorts.
I told him it was none of his business how I dressed and to never message me again.
Bitch. You're just lucky I'm a fucking gentleman.

I was the one dressed provocatively in an unsupervised multi-purpose room.
He was the one with the uncommon decency not to act on his urges.
I should be thanking him, right?

When I was 16, I was sexually assaulted by a graduating senior.
I didn't tell anyone,
because it took me three years to realize he did anything wrong.

When I was 18, I was sexually assaulted in my dorm room my first week of college.
The police officer told me to *be careful.*
You don't want to ruin the rest of a young man's life.
Then he asked how much pot I smoked.

My rapist graduated college in 2015.
They expelled me for attempting suicide in my dorm room before the end of my first semester.
He's gone on to become a high-profile political journalist who covers, among other things, the MeToo movement.
I've gone on to become a Title IX activist.

At 21, I was sexually assaulted for the third time, by a man with a service position at a support group I attended for young people in recovery. In order to get ahead of the story, he told his girlfriend I came onto him and he rejected me.
At our next fellowship meeting, I got hit with a *You can't sit with us.*
By another 21-year-old woman. Someone I considered a friend.
I never went back.

The thing is, when you're conditioned from your formative years to believe that your ownership over your body is secondary to boys' entertainment, you stop understanding you have a right to the word 'No.'

When no one tells you you don't have to let people touch you when you don't want them to, you never learn when it crosses from annoyance to felony.

If you think children shouldn't be taught about consent, my guess is you've also made one or more of the following statements. See if any of these sound like you:

"They're too young to understand."
"Rape isn't a culture!"
"If it really happened, she would've reported it back then."
"With all this MeToo stuff, how do you we know where 'the line' is anymore?"

It's not hard. You don't have to graph it
based on its fucking derivative.
But if you're genuinely asking, let's clear it up right now.
Are you ready?
It's advanced stuff. You may want to write this down.

THE. LINE. IS. WHEREVER. SOMEONE. FUCKING. DRAWS. IT.

Clear enough?
If you're still confused, read it again.
If a person tells you they don't want to be touched,

DON'T. FUCKING. TOUCH. THEM.

Imagine, for a second, I told you someone stole my TV.
Would you ask me who was permitted to push its buttons? Who basked in its blue halo before it disappeared? Would it matter who I'd invited into my home to watch the channels change?
No, it wouldn't.
Because it was my TV, and someone took it without my consent.

So if you've ever asked a survivor what they consented to prior to being assaulted, the question you really need to be asking yourself is: *why do you value the sanctity of ownership over an inanimate object more than you value a person's ownership of their own body?*

This is only a gendered issue to the extent that we make it one. We teach girls that violation of their space is a sign of affection. Then we shame women for not saying something sooner. Where is "the line" in all of the stories you just read?

Did I have a right to my discomfort when I felt trapped at 8?

When there was ball sweat on my pencil case at 12?

When I was assaulted for the 3rd time at 21?

What about now?

I had a right to boundaries the first time someone put their hands on me in a way I didn't want. I should've been taught how to tell people when I didn't want to be touched, not given reasons to justify it.
If we don't start teaching kids this now, we're just handing another generation the same excuses we keep hearing today:

"I didn't know they didn't want it."
"They should've said something when it happened."
"They were asking for it."

I don't know about you, but I'm tired of these excuses.

In every single class I've taught, I've had at least one student come to me with some variety of,
Miss Katya, So-and-so keeps touching me!

And every time my response is,
Did you tell So-and-so that you didn't like that?

Every instance of unwanted touching I've encountered as an educator ends in one of two ways:
Either the touch-er needs help putting on their listening ears, or the touch-ee needs help finding the right words to express,
No thank you, I need some space right now.

I have yet to teach a child who has failed to grasp this concept, and I've worked with toddlers to adolescents.

It's adults who seem to have the most trouble.

What you're really saying if you think children don't understand consent is that *you* don't understand it.

And if that's the case, I'm more than happy to teach you.

Put on your fucking listening ears. You're old enough.

Respectfully,

A Very Tired Teacher

persona poem as a $10 mason jar full of screws
at some hipster store in Toronto

Look, I didn't ask to be here either.

I don't deny being useless at
most non-whimsical pursuits
but consider how jarring
this has been for me

I just want to be among old books and soft wood and settling dust
consider the archetypal energy of oxidizing metal
and like, develop my aesthetic

yet suddenly I'm expected
to partake in this capitalist hellscape to continue existing—
how can I help it if my only marketable parts
are sharp edges and fragility?

(they want me hard enough to handle being screwed
but they need to see how easily I can be made to shatter)

The tarot deck on my shelf thinks
I must have the same moon & rising signs:
Probably Cancer, she says, maybe Virgo
I stare back, glassy-eyed. I say,

*It's probably neither because I am a jarful of screws
& therefore largely unaffected by celestial bodies.*

a rising sign is just the vessel, she says,
the moon sign means your insides

but I say there's no difference
between container and contained
in my unending display of insides

she says *That's what I'm telling you, you translucent bitch*

& my insides can only say in answer

SCREW
(you)

?

Palinode re: suicide notes by the author

I've been thinking how every poem I write is a suicide note—

the way a caged bird's scream
comes out in song

the way shackles are just bracelets
until you learn the word for freedom.

There are months I've been alive
only for not having written a good enough goodbye yet.
It isn't much, but it's a reason to stay.

Once a man in a white lab coat read to me from my own Xeroxed
handwriting

      THINK OF ME HAPPY IF YOU THINK OF ME AT ALL

& asked what gave me the right to take my own life.

I asked him what gave him the right to read other people's letters.

There's something so incredibly American
about violently tethering a human being to an unwanted existence
and saying *This is yours now.*

This thing you never asked for
this thing you do not want
& we will take your freedom
& your shoelaces
& the underwire in your underwear

until you accept it is yours.
But not yours to take.
Understand?

I've been thinking how anyone can be a cautionary tale
but being an inspiration demands
redemption.

Nowadays everyone wants me
to be a spokesperson for existing

like, aren't the bars on a birdcage
the same tune as the bars in birdsong?

& am I not so *grateful*
to the fluorescent lights
& the air forced back into my deflated lungs

& the EMTs
pulling lightning from the October sky
& Zeus's hands on my chest
shocking my defenseless heart into stirring?
Do I not want to kiss the ground that found my feet
when they dragged me back screaming from the abyss?

& it's true most days I don't count exits
but I still feel them
vestigial organs in a wet skeleton:

> THERE IS NO HAPPINESS.
> THERE IS ONLY PAIN AND LESS PAIN.

Once my mother, in a halo of fluorescent lights,
told me I loved no one, her voice a scalpel
& in answer I drew from my pocket:

> I HAVE NOT DONE, NOR WILL I DO,
> ANYTHING IN SUCH A SHORT AND SELFISH LIFE
> TO DESERVE THE LOVE I HAVE RECEIVED.

The only difference between a poem and a suicide note
is what you do when you put down the pen.

It gets easier
is a necessary lie,
we just get used to the pain

but I've been thinking how every poem ever written is a suicide note—
a shout into an eternal silence, a sandprint made by a fist

a mark that says *This*
is how I would have you think of me.
This is proof I lived & bled & took up space here.

This is what will remain of my life when I have gone
& spent every red and incredible second of it.

THIS IS ALL I'VE LOVED & SWALLOWED & HURT &

HURT & SAVED & BURNED

& BORROWED

&

;

a list of musical ephemera I identify with more than any gender

—the instrumental bit at the end of *Canyon Moon*, the third-to-last track on Harry Styles' second album, played on a bespoke mountain dulcimer built by the same hands as Joni Mitchell's on *Blue*

—that part in Frank Zappa's *Muffin Man*, where he says *sterile canvas snoot of a fully-charged icing anointment utensil* all ominously, cracks up as though realizing for the first time what a ridiculous fucking lyric that is, then goes, "let's try that again," does it over with greater commitment, and uses the entire take in the studio version

—when Eric Clapton made that entire album wailing in his basement after George Harrison's ex-wife left him for George Harrison

—when Bob Dylan said, "this here ain't no protest song or anything like that, 'cause I don't write no protest songs," then played *Blowin' in the Wind*

—when a guy I'd just met called me Basic for naming *Lithium* as my favorite Nirvana song, and then failed to recognize the lyrics from its first verse tattooed on my bicep

—the way I listened to that song on repeat in the psych ward at 18 before they took my headphones away in case I tried wrapping them around my throat, how those simple chords got me through all the days without sunlight, how I spent most of my adolescence convinced nobody but Kurt would ever understand me

—whatever soul-rocking song the river is singing in 'Brokedown Palace,' that Jerry Garcia keeps telling us to listen to in the chorus

—a rocking-horse person eating marshmallow pie on the bridge beside the fountain in the second verse of *Lucy in the Sky with Diamonds*

—I could write essays on the significance of a single vowel in Jeff Buckley's colloquial interpretation of Leonard Cohen's lyrics: how rhyming "do 'ya?"

with 'Hallelujah' transformed a lofty ballad into a soft-rock classic that lent gritty, kitchen-sink realism to stark, ecclesiastical imagery / how this implied juxtaposition of run-of-the-mill heartache with archetypal tragedy creates a textured emotional resonance / as though to love and to lose are lenses by the highest stakes of human condition become universally accessible

—those liminal seconds as a song fades to nothing, when all that's left is a purple whisper of vibration / & it feels holy, like the edges of the world melt and remake themselves in the absence of self, & it's there / bobbing like a cork in this silence that you see / the music has been inside you all along / & every song ever written is just a jumble of chords / broken off the music of spheres / all life is made from, and this thing we call art / is just the unclogging of a vessel / & how silly it makes us / to hang any of our hats / on the rambling of any single mortal coil / when consciousness is, by its own definition / limitless

—the little *ooOOOOooo* in the background of the bridge to *High Road*, the lead single from Broken Bells' self-titled debut (a supergroup collaboration between James Mercer of The Shins and artist-producer Brian Burton, better known as Danger Mouse)

it's too late to change your mind / you let loss / be your guide

in which the author tries to explain what the deal is with queer millenials and Harry Styles

I can't explain it
      except

have you ever seen
a leaf
in an arc of wind,

suspended
at the opening notes
of fall?

when fresh-dew summer
still clings

blue-green
to the stem?

burning harvest

waiting soft
& urgent as memory,

to cross earth's threshold
to cease & become
& become again
to feed the flowers growing there
like the dying
of dusk sets fire to

a cathedral window—
daisies, sunflowers,
reaching, open
in unpretentious beauty:
there is, I suppose,
something awe-inspiring

about anything

that defies its own labeling
that, gifted a world
where they can be anything,
refuses the choosing, chooses
& chooses again

                                  to be themselves.

Space-cows Struggle with Transitions to factory farming

Johnny is 5¾ years old.
His first week in my after-school poetry class
he writes about a space-cow who swallows the moon.
Second week, Johnny scowls
when I call his name on the roll sheet. *My* name *is Jonathan*, he says.

The Artist Formerly Known as Johnny's daytime-teacher, it turns out, has
renamed him 'Jonathan' because there's already another Johnny in his
class. Now he's afraid he'll get in trouble for being called by his name.

My first teaching job requires an MD's signature on a negative TB test.
Are you on any medication? she asks.
I name the pills I swallowed at breakfast. *I see.*

Her tone grows cold, clinical, under a thin veneer of softness, like the
papery examination table that moments before held my bare body.

What is your diagnosis?

I tell her I am ~~unfit to supervise children~~.
At least, this is what she hears.
It doesn't matter what I say next.

*

I am working with Johnny on a story about a spider-dinosaur hybrid.
He's got big, dark eyes that light up when he invents new animals.
But he doesn't like it when you look into them.
If you try to, he'll stop talking.

*

I'm 10 years old & Mrs. Carr makes me sit at my desk with my head down
for 15 minutes when I get too excited.

You're like a little butterfly, she says. *And you need to learn how to be a
quiet little butterfly.*

I ask her what a loud butterfly sounds like.
She doesn't care for this question.

Two behavioral therapists shadow Johnny, scribbling on clipboards.
He takes a Lego block and pushes against the inside of a blue marker cap
while he looks for words. Click. It sticks out on both ends. He does it
again. Click.
The block doesn't fit. Click.

Useless.
Lost cause.
Click. The clipboards don't care for fidgeting. *Quiet hands.*
Click. *Eyes on the teacher, Jonathan.*
Click, click, click. *Pay attention, Jonathan.* Click.
They take away his marker.
Quiet hands.

*

Do you want to draw your story instead? I ask. A nod.
I hand him a new marker.
Clipboards fill in pages of charts with numbers while watching him work.

Nico says the spider-saur has 10,000 legs all over his body.
Nico knows how to count to 10,000.
They do not write this down.

*

I am 15 years old & I don't like the blue pills
or the way they make my brain spin.
Clipboards name me *Non-compliant.* Oppositional to the point of
pathology.
Willfully defiant.
Entitled.
Immature.

Something takes hold in my body, like an itch, a restlessness.

I am kneeling in wet shards before I remember deciding to break the glass.

*

Left clipboard asks me to stand up. Takes my seat.
Tiny shoulders tense.
He knows he is being tested.
They ask questions to help us assimilate.

*

I am dripping, shaking, bleeding. Picking up the pieces of something that looks like it never fit in the first place.
I catch my distorted reflection in a pinkish puddle on the tile floor.
Useless.
Lost cause.

*

Clipboard interrupts Johnny Jonathan's story to ask,
"How would you feel if you saw a dinosaur in real life?"

How would you *feel if you had to abandon the creature you were imagining to answer unimaginative questions, assessing your ability to imagine shit?*

How do you expect anyone to build understanding when you take away their tools?

*

Next class I tell Johnny *Use your imagination.*
He says he doesn't have one.

He says I can't hold a pencil right.
At the back of the classroom, a pencil scratches a clipboard.

Friday I have a talk with my director, and my classroom becomes a
clipboard-free zone.
I tell my poets

it's okay to move around if that's how your brain works best.
it's okay if you listen better while your hands are busy.
it's okay to be scared of new people.

and I crawl under the desk with him so he hears.

You come out when you feel safe.
You speak when you are ready.

You don't have to be Jonathan if you don't want to.

You can be whoever you want here.

But how do I teach them to be themselves

in a world that takes their own name from their mouth
and spits back a new one?

*

Not fitting in is not the same as unfit
but this world
would rather carve the edges off every square peg
than ask itself why all the holes are round.

*

But I will teach them we can paint portraits of ourselves with just words
& not one of them has to be a diagnosis.
You can learn all the ways your brain will try to trick you,
and still trust yourself.

& when it feels
like this world has taken all that is left of you,
I will be here
to listen
and understand
and see you as you are:

here, we can be whoever we want.

self-portrait as a CVS bag impaled by a tree branch in an arlington heights parking lot

i should've known a need to be useful
means getting yourself used.
but would you see me the same if you knew
before my insides were zoloft and sugar-
free Red Bull they were nothing at all?

it's not emptiness i run from.
it's nothingness
inside empty places
       up here
where my ribbon innards flutter transparent in frozen silence
where bald twigs drag fingernail revolts, spine bent
across slate-leveled skies, i can see (i've often said i do my best

thinking in trees) why
letting go makes
more litterer of you
than garbage of me.

they said i was made too delicate
to hold, but maybe they meant they resented my
transparency (how i could not hide the way i contained

everything they didn't want to carry for themselves), how i stretched
to accommodate baggage i was never made to know the weight of

until it tore right through me, how they mistook
my flexibility for fragility). but let me explain:

i am only as disposable as you make me

even split clean through my middle, undisturbed, i
could watch ages of men rise and fall like the breaking
of dawn every day from this tree and outlast them all

simply by refusing to be degraded.
& i never wanted you to save me
only to know if i could fly...

it doesn't much matter who
or what made me, only
what i've made of myself & maybe

i'd be lying if i said i didn't miss your touch
that i wouldn't say with the same smile to
HAVE A NICE DAY☺
if i saw you go by, but once

i cried for fifteen minutes in a strip mall parking spot to the musical
stylings of Jeff Buckley

as i watched the wind
rapture my body from the pavement (y'all,
i'd never been touched so gently)

than this certain, wistful something in the way i
grazed that pigeon carcass by the bus stop
rose with such haunting grace

to kiss the awning
of the 24-hour laundromat.

one day, you'll see me
carried like a sorrowful note
along a winter's breath, listen

for the feeble fluttering
of air in polyethylene
& hear only

my unbroken
hallelujah.

Gratitudes

Josh at Game Over Books, for believing in this collection before it made any sense, helping it become what it is today, and helping keep it a reasonable length despite the Zinn law of first drafts.

My editor Story for understanding and valuing the message behind my work, tolerating endless discussions of semicolon placement and em-dash merit (and making every poem in here better for it), and for being a shining example of nominative determinism (and giving me an excuse to use the phrase). Oh also, for fixing (most of) my run-on sentences.

Catherine Weiss for the incredible cover design.

Ilyus and Maya for being the kindest, most generous blurbin' outfitters I ever could've hoped for.

Dr. Elyn Saks, for your bravery, activism, and inspiration.

The incredible team of educators I'm lucky enough to call both friends and colleagues, for your support, guidance, thought-provoking conversation, and ability to create a space that inspires me personally and professionally every day.

Every teacher who ever said, *keep writing* and made me believe my stories were worth telling: Mrs. Bramer, Mrs. Fuhrman, Amy, Bernie, Professor Sanders, and Professor Smith, to name just a few.

Harry Styles for getting me through quarantine and being a style icon.

My fairy godmother Lyn/Nina/Niner 49-er, for always having my back, and being one of the strongest women I know.

My parents for growing me in a test tube and encouraging me to follow my dreams.

My brother Leif for shouldering the burden of being the sane sibling through many revolving doors of hospitals and institutions.

My friend Sam, for encouraging me to be myself and be better at the same time, teaching me the importance of being Seen, listening to endless info-dumps about Chuck E. Cheese, and for everything you've ever told me... mostly the stuff about yogurt.

My best friend/sister Anna, for laughing with me at the stuff we're not supposed to laugh about, saving my life more than once in more than one way, and for making me the cool aunt. Special shoutout to Jack, Atticus, Charlotte, and Aiobhean—the greatest family to ever come out of the roof of a tire shop.

The Pass-on Problems crew: Abigail, Mikayla, Eliza, Sarah (rest in peace, our Ace of Sunshine) for showing me the meaning of true friendship, just when I'd lost faith it existed, and for making that fluorescently-lit hallway feel like a home.

Blaise and Sara, for helping me survive my brain.

All of Bill's friends, for showing me a spiritual path and a life worth living.

My uncle Lennard & Aunt Sonny, for the unconditional love, and for listening without making me feel crazy.

My students, for teaching me that empathy requires only recognizing someone's emotional reality to be as vivid and complex as one's own. And more new types of Pokemon than I'll ever be able to remember.

Aaron H.—don't worry, you're not "Boy." I love our ships-in-the-night friendship, I do have hobbies, and I'm slightly less melodramatic in real life than poems. I just liked the story about pickles. It arrived at a deeper truth somehow.

Jake "Clarke" Hoskins, the first person to call me a Manic Pixie Dream Girl. If this somehow finds its way to you, I have a proper amends, if you're ever ready to hear it. I'm sorry we've only known each other at our worst.

Margy—your feminist credentials are irrevocable. Your bravery is unequivocal.

Everyone I've ever befriended on a grippy sock vacation: Thank you. I love you. I'm glad you're alive.

Melanie, Maria, and Vivian at Mariposa: you're the reason I made it. "Thank you" doesn't begin to cover it.

Sam the paramedic: you found me in the ICU TV room, high-fived me for hobbling myself in with just a walker, sat down next to me, and went, "Sorry I ruined your suicide attempt," and it's still the funniest fucking thing anyone's ever said to me

And finally, to Mr. Charles E. Cheese: thank you for being the hero I didn't know I needed, and the Saint we don't deserve

Acknowledgments

A prior version of "Pickled" appeared in the Fall 2017 issue of *The Merrimack Review*.

A prior version of "self-portrait as a CVS bag impaled by a tree branch in an arlington heights parking lot" was published in Issue 9.2 of *Underground*.

The line "How do you expect anyone to build understanding when you take away their tools?" in "Space-cows Struggle with Transitions to factory farming" was adapted from a line by Emil Eastman in the original group piece of the same name.

The lines "You help people heal, and a ton of them / owe you their lives. I / just never asked / to be one of them" from "Salt Lake City, Utah has the world's largest collection of horned dinosaur fossils" and "every man who heard *Try harder* / when I told him *No*" from "In an alternate universe where it really is a scary time for men" were inspired by two Brenna Twohy performances: "Open Letter from Rescue Annie to the Norwegian Toymaker Asmund Laerdal" and "Fantastic Breasts and Where to Find Them." Thank you Brenna for your work, and your inspiration.

Biography

Katya Zinn is a Boston-based, LA-born-and-raised performance poet, educator, and activist. Their first chapbook-length collection human verses was released in 2021. When not shouting poems to mostly-strangers at local dives, she works as a teaching artist and equity director of a children's education nonprofit, where she's working on starting a scholarship program to provide free therapeutic mentorship in the arts to neurodivergent children from low-income backgrounds. Zinn is currently the self-appointed poet laureate of Chuck E. Cheese, but hopes to make the title official (as soon as she can get Charles to respond to one of her tweets). Manic-depressive Pixie Dream Girl is her first full-length collection. Whilst writing it, she (in a manner reminiscent of a film-noir detective pinning yarn to a wall of photos before he loses his badge for being Too Close To The Case), created the following visual aid, then proceeded to annoy her editor about it until he finally agreed to put it somewhere in the book.

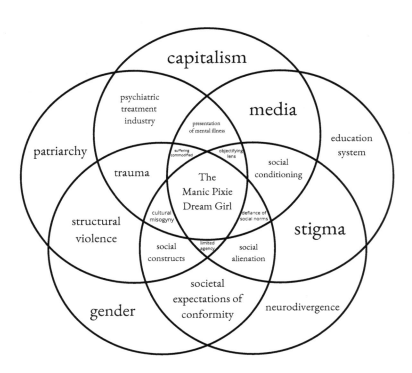